D1416069

THE BURNING-GLASS

New Poems, including THE TRAVELLER

BY THE SAME AUTHOR

BELLS AND GRASS

MEMOIRS OF A MIDGET

PEACOCK PIE

THE LISTENERS AND OTHER POEMS

THE

URNING - LASS

AND OTHER POEMS

INCLUDING

THE TRAVELLER

BY

WALTER DE LA MARE

THE VIKING PRESS

NEW YORK

1945

SEDES SAPIENTIAE LIBRARY
DOMINICAN COLLEGE OF BLAUVELT, N. Y.

DISCARDED

33423

Copyright 1945 by Walter de la Mare
Published by the Viking Press in October 1945
THE TRAVELLER has been published in
a separate volume in England

Designed by Stefan Salter
Manufactured in U.S.A. by H. Wolff, New York, N. Y.

CONTENTS

The poems in the following collection have various origins in time, mood, and place. Some of them were written many years ago, and have since been revised; others recently. My gratitude is due to the Editors of the periodicals in which several of them first appeared.

THE BURNING-GLASS

A PORTRAIT

Old; yet unchanged:—still pottering in his thoughts;
Still eagerly enslaved by books and print;
Less plagued, perhaps, by rigid musts and oughts,
But no less frantic in vain argument;

Still happy as a child, with its small toys,
Over his inkpot and his bits and pieces—
Life's arduous, fragile and ingenuous joys,
Whose charm failed never—nay, it even increases;

Ev'n happier in watch of bird or flower,
Rainbow in heaven, or bud on thorny spray,
A star-strewn nightfall, and that heart-break hour
Of sleep-drowsed senses between dawn and day;

Loving, the light—laved eyes in those wild hues!—
And dryad twilight, and the thronging dark;
A Crusoe ravished by mere solitude—
And silence—edged with music's faintest *Hark!*

And any chance-seen face whose loveliness
Hovers, a mystery, between dream and real;
Things usual yet miraculous that bless
And overwell a heart that still can feel;

Haunted by questions no man answered yet;
Pining to leap from A clean on to Z;
Absorbed by problems which the wise forget;
Avid for fantasy—yet how staid a head!

[3]

Senses at daggers with his intellect;
Quick, stupid; vain, retiring; ardent, cold;
Faithful and fickle; rash and circumspect;
And never yet at rest in any fold;

Punctual at meals; a spendthrift, close as Scot;
Rebellious, tractable, childish—long gone grey!
Impatient, volatile, tongue wearying not—
Loose, too: which, yet, thank heaven, was taught to pray;

"Childish" indeed!—a waif on shingle shelf
Fronting the rippled sands, the sun, the sea;
And nought but his marooned precarious self
For questing consciousness and will-to-be;

A feeble venturer—in a world so wide!
So rich in action, daring, cunning, strife!
You'd think, poor soul, he had taken Sloth for bride—
Unless the imagined is the breath of life;

Unless to speculate bring virgin gold,
And *Let's pretend* can range the seven seas,
And dreams are not mere tales by idiot told,
And tongueless truth may hide in fantasies:

Unless the alone may their own company find,
And churchyards harbour phantoms 'mid their bones,
And even a daisy may suffice a mind
Whose bindweed can redeem a heap of stones;

[4]

Too frail a basket for so many eggs—
Loose-woven: Gosling? cygnet? Laugh or weep?
Or is the cup at richest in its dregs?
The actual reallest on the verge of sleep?

One yet how often the prey of doubt and fear,
Of bleak despondence, stark anxiety;
Ardent for what is neither now nor here,
An Orpheus fainting for Eurydice;

Not yet inert, but with a tortured breast
At hint of that bleak gulf—his last farewell;
Pining for peace, assurance, pause and rest,
Yet slave to what he loves past words to tell;

A foolish, fond old man, his bed-time nigh,
Who still at western window stays to win
A transient respite from the latening sky,
And scarce can bear it when the Sun goes in.

IN THE LOCAL MUSEUM

They stood—rain pelting at window, shrouded sea—
Tenderly hand in hand, too happy to talk;
And there, its amorous eye intent on me,
Plautus impennis, the extinct Great Auk.

THE RAPIDS

Grieve must my heart. Age hastens by.
No longing can stay Time's torrent now.
Once would the sun in eastern sky
Pause on the solemn mountain's brow.
Rare flowers he still to bloom may bring,
But day approaches evening;
And ah, how swift their withering!

The birds, that used to sing, sang then
As if in an eternal day;
Ev'n sweeter yet their grace notes, when
Farewell . . . farewell is theirs to say.
Yet, as a thorn its drop of dew
Treasures in shadow, crystal clear,
All that I loved I love anew,
  Now parting draweth near.

ARIEL

Ariel! Ariel!—
But the glittering moon
Sank to the curve of the world,
Down, down:
And the curlew cried,
And the nightjar stirred in her rest,
And Ariel on the cool high steep of heaven
Leaned his breast.

Ariel! Ariel!—
His curv'd wings whist,
With the bliss of the star-shaking breeze
'Gainst his pinions prest.
Lower the great globe
Rolled her icy snows:
Lone is the empty dark, and the moonless heart
When the Bright One goes.

THE SUMMONS

"What bodiless bird so wildly sings,
Albeit from no earthly tree?
Whence rise again those Phoenix wings
To waken from prolonged unease—
Isle of the Lost Hesperides!
  A self long strange to me?"

"Red coral in the sea may shine,
And rock-bound Sirens, half divine,
Seduced Ulysses: but to find
Music as rare as childhood's thrush
Yet lorn as curlew's at the hush
  Of dewfall in the mind!"

"O shallow questioner! Know you not
That notes like these, sad, urgent, sweet,
Call from an Egypt named the heart,
Which with a deeper life doth beat
Than any wherein thought hath part;
And of whose wisdom, Love knows well,
  Only itself could tell?"

A DULL BOY

"Work?" Well, not *work*—this stubborn desperate quest
To conjure life, love, wonder into words;
Far happier songs than any me have blest
Were sung, at ease, this daybreak by the birds.

I watch with breathless envy in her glass
The dreamlike beauty of the silent swan;
As mute a marvel is the bladed grass
Springing to life again, June's sickle gone.

What music could be mine compared with that
The idling wind woos from the sand-dune's bent?
What meaning deeper than the smile whereat
A burning heart conceives the loved intent?

"And what did'st *thou*" . . . I see the vaulted throng,
The listening heavens in that dread array
Fronting the Judge to whom all dooms belong:—
Will the lost child in me cry bravely, "Play"?

TWO GARDENS

Two gardens see!—this, of enchanted flowers,
Strange to the eye, and more than earthly-sweet;
Small rivulets running, song-reëchoing bowers;
And green-walled pathways which, ere parting, meet;
And there a lion-like sun in heaven's delight
Breathes plenitude from dayspring to the night.

The other:—walls obscure, and chaces of trees—
Ilex and yew, and dream-enticing dark,
Hid pools, moths, creeping odours, silentness,
Luna its deity, and its watchword, *Hark!*
A still and starry mystery, wherein move
Phantoms of ageless wonder and of love.

Two gardens for two children—in one mind:
But ah, how seldom open now their gates I find!

NOSTALGIA

In the strange city of life
A house I know full well—
That wherein Silence a refuge has,
Where Dark doth dwell.

Gable and roof it stands,
Fronting the dizzied street,
Where Vanity flaunts her gilded booths
In the noontide glare and heat.

Green-graped upon its walls
Earth's ancient hoary vine
Clusters the carven lichenous stone
With tendril serpentine.

Deafened, incensed, dismayed,
Dazed in the clamorous throng,
I thirst for the soundless fount that rills
As if from my inmost heart, and fills
The stillness with its song.

As yet I knock in vain:
Nor yet what is hidden can tell;
Where Silence perpetual vigil keeps,
Where Dark doth dwell.

THE SECRET

I bless the hand that once held mine,
 The lips that said:
"No heart, though kiss were Circe's wine,
 Can long be comforted."

Ay, though we talked the long day out
 Of all life marvels at,
One thing the soul can utter not,
 Or self to self relate.

We gaze, enravished, you and I,
 Like children at a flower;
But speechless stayed, past even a sigh . . .
 Not even Babel Tower

Heard language strange and close enough
 To tell that moment's peace,
Where broods the Phoenix, timeless Love,
 And divine silence is.

WINTER COMPANY

Blackbird silent in the snow;
Motionless crocus in the mould;
Naked tree; and, cold and low,
        Sun's wintry gold . . .

Lost for the while in their strange beauty—self how far!—
Lulled were my senses into a timeless dream;
As if the inmost secret of what they are
        Lay open in what they seem.

THE SOLITARY BIRD

Why should a bird in that solitary hollow
    Flying from east to west
Seém in the silence of the snow-blanched sunshine
    Gilding the valley's crest
Envoy and symbol of a past within me
    Centuries now at rest?
Shallowly arched the horizon looms beyond it,
    Turquoise green and blue;
Not even a whisper irks the magic of the evening
    The narrowing valley through;
No faintest echo brings a syllable revealing
    The secret once I knew:
Down *whsts* the snow again, cloud masks the sunshine—
    Bird gone, and memory too.

"Night-night, my Precious!"; "*Sweet* dreams, Sweet!"
"Heaven bless you, Child!"—the accustomed grown-ups said.
Two eyes gazed mutely back that none could meet,
Then turned to face Night's terrors overhead.

ISRAFEL

(To Alec McLaren)

1940

Sleepless I lay, as the grey of dawn
Through the cold void street stole into the air,
When, in the hush, a solemn voice
Pealed suddenly out in Connaught Square.

Had I not heard notes wild as these
A thousand times in childhood ere
This chill March daybreak they awoke
The echoing walls of Connaught Square,

I might have imagined a seraph—strange
In such bleak days!—had deigned to share,
For joy and love, the haunts of man—
An Israfel in Connaught Square!

Not that this singer eased the less
A human heart surcharged with care—
Merely a blackbird, London-bred,
Warbling of Spring in Connaught Square!

It was the contrast with a world
Of darkness, horror, grief, despair,
Had edged with an irony so sharp
That rapturous song in Connaught Square.

[17]

HARVEST HOME

A bird flies up from the hayfield;
Sweet, to distraction, is the new-mown grass:
But I grieve for its flowers laid low at noonday—
    And only this poor *Alas!*

I grieve for War's innocent lost ones—
The broken loves, the mute goodbye,
The dread, the courage, the bitter end,
The shaken faith, the glazing eye?

O bird, from the swathes of that hayfield—
The rancid stench of the grass!
And a heart stricken mute by that Harvest Home—
    And only this poor *Alas!*

THE UNUTTERABLE

(September 1940)

What! jibe in ignorance, and scold
The Muses when, the earth in flame,
They hold their peace, and leave untolled
Ev'n Valour's deathless requiem?

Think you a heart in misery,
Riven with pity, dulled with woe,
Could weep in song its threnody,
And to such tombs with chauntings go?

Think you that all-abandoning deeds
Of sacrifice by those whose love
Must barren lie in widow's weeds,
Gone all their youth was dreaming of,

Can be revealed in words? Alas!
No poet yet in Fate's dark count
Has ever watched Night dread as this,
Or seen such evils to surmount.

We stand aghast. Pride, rapture, grief
In storm within; on fire to bless
The daybreak; but yet wiser if
We bide that hour in silentness.

THE SPECTACLE

Scan with calm bloodshot eyes the world around us,
Its broken stones, its sorrows! No voice could tell
The toll of the innocent crucified, weeping and wailing,
In this region of torment ineffable, flame and derision,
    What wonder if we believe no longer in Hell?

    And Heaven? That daybreak vision?
In the peace of our hearts we learn beyond shadow of doubting
That our dream of this vanished kingdom lies sleeping
    within us;
Its gates are the light we have seen in the hush of the morning,
When the shafts of the sunrise break in a myriad splendours;
Its shouts of joy are those of all earthly creatures,
Their primal and innocent language—the song of the birds:
Thrush in its rapture, ecstatic wren, and wood-dove tender,
Calling on us poor mortals to put our praise into words.

Passionate, sorrowful hearts, too—the wise, the true and
    the gentle;
Minds that outface all fear, defy despair, remain faithful,
Endure in silence, hope on, assured in their selfless courage,
Natural and sweet in a love no affliction or doubt could dispel.

If, as a glass reflecting its range, we have these for our guidance,
If, as our love creates beauty, we exult in that transient
    radiance,
This is the garden of paradise which in our folly
    We abandoned long ages gone.

Though, then, the wondrous divine were ev'n nebulae-distant,
The little we make of our all is our earthly heaven.
  Else we are celled in a darkness,
Windowless, doorless, alone.

AN ISLAND

Parched, panting, he awoke; phantasmal light
Blueing the hollows of his fevered eyes;
And strove to tell of what he had dreamed that night—
In stumbling words its meaning to devise:—

An island, lit with beauty, like a flower
Its sea of sapphire fringed with driven snow,
Whose music and beauty with the changing hour
Seemed from some inward source to ebb and flow;
A heart, all innocence and innately wise,
Well-spring of very love appeared to be—
"A candle whose flame," he stammered, "never dies,
But feeds on light itself perpetually.
Me! This! A thing corrupt on the grave's cold brink,
And into outer darkness soon to sink!"

The tired nurse yawned. "A queer dream that!" she said.
"But now you are awake. And see, it's day."
She smoothed the pillow for his sweat-dark head,
Muttered, "There, sleep again!" and turned away.

THE SCARECROW

In the abandoned orchard—on a pole,
The rain-soaked trappings of that scarecrow have
Usurped the semblance of a man—poor soul—
    Haled from a restless grave.

Geese for his company this fog-bound noon,
He eyeless stares. And I with eyes reply.
Lifting a snakelike head, the gander yelps
    " 'Ware!" at the passer-by.

It is as though a few bedraggled rags
Poised in this wintry waste were lure enough
To entice some aimless phantom here to mime
    All it is image of . . .

Once Man in grace divine all beauty was;
And of his bone God made a lovelier Eve;
Now even the seraphs sleep at sentry-go;
    The swine break in to thieve

Wind-fallen apples from the two old Trees.
Oh see, Old Adam, once of Eden! Alas!
How is thy beauty fallen: fallen thine Eve,
    Who did all life surpass!

Should in the coming nightfall the Lord God,
Goose-challenged, call, "My Creature, where art *thou*?"
Scarecrow of hate and vengeance, wrath and blood,
    What would'st thou answer now?

[23]

THE BURNING-GLASS

No map shows my Jerusalem,
　　No history my Christ;
Another language tells of them,
　　A hidden evangelist.

Words may create rare images
　　Within their narrow bound;
'Twas speechless childhood brought me these,
　　As music may, in sound.

Yet not the loveliest song that ever
　　Died on the evening air
Could from my inmost heart dissever
　　What life had hidden there.

It is the blest reminder of
　　What earth in shuddering bliss
Nailed on a cross—that deathless Love
　　Through all the eternities.

I am the Judas whose perfidy
　　Sold what no eye hath seen,
The rabble in dark Gethsemane,
　　And Mary Magdalene.

To very God who day and night
　　Tells me my sands out-run,
I cry in misery infinite,
　　"I am thy long-lost son."

EDGES

Think you your heart is safely at rest,
Contemptuous, calm, disdainful one?
Maybe a stone is in your breast
   From whence all motion's gone.

Undauntable soldier, vent no scorn
On him who in terror faced the foe;
There is a radiant core of rapture
   None but the fearful know.

And you, sweet poet? Heaven might kiss
The miracles you dreamed to do;
But waste not your soul on self-sought bliss,
   Since no such dream comes true.

SWIFTS

No; they are only birds—swifts, in the loft of the morning,
Coursing, disporting, courting, in the pale-blue arc of the sky.
There is no venom for kin or for kind in their wild-winged
    archery,
Nor death in their innocent droppings as fleet in their mansions
    they fly;
Swooping, with flicker of pinion to couple, the loved with
    the loved one,
Never with malice or hate, in their vehement sallies
    through space.
Listen! that silken rustle, as they charge on their beehive
    houses,
Fashioned of dried-up mud daubed each in its chosen place.
Hunger—not fear—sharps the squawk of their featherless
    nestlings;
From daybreak into the dark their circuitings will not cease:
How beautiful they!—and the feet on earth's heavenly moun-
    tains
Of him that bringeth good tidings, proclaimeth the gospel
    of peace!

THE VISITANT

A little boy leaned down his head
   Upon his mother's knee;
"Tell me the old, old tale," he said,
   "You told last night to me."

It was in dream. For when at dawn
   She woke, and raised her head,
Still haunted her sad face forlorn
   The beauty of the dead.

THE FIELD

Yes, there was once a battle here:
There, where the grass takes on a shade
Of paradisal green, sun-clear—
   There the last stand was made.

LULLAY

"Now lullay, my sweeting,
What hast thou to fear?
It is only the wind
In the willows we hear,
And the sigh of the waves
By the sand dunes, my dear.
Stay thy wailing. Let sleep be
Thy solace, thou dear;
And dreams that shall charm
From that cheek every tear.
See, see, I am with thee
No harm can come near.
Sleep, sleep, then, my loved one,
My lorn one, my dear!" . . .

I heard that far singing
With pining oppressed,
When grief for one absent
My bosom distressed,
When the star of the evening
Was low in the West.
And I mused as I listened,
With sorrow oppressed,
Would that heart were *my* pillow,
That safety my rest!
Ah, would I could slumber—

A child laid to rest—
Could abide but a moment
Assoiled, on that breast,
While the planet of evening
Sinks low in the west:
Could wake, and dream on,
At peace and at rest;
Ere fall the last darkness,
When silence is best.

For alas, love is mortal;
And night must come soon;
And another, yet deeper,
When—no more to roam—
The lost one within me
Shall find its long home,
In a sleep none can trouble,
The hush of the tomb.

Cold, sombre, eternal,
Dark, narrow that room;
But no grief, no repining
Will deepen its gloom;
Though of voice, once adored,
Not an echo can come;
Of hand, brow, and cheek,
My rapture and doom,
Once my all, and adored,
No least phantom can come. . . .

"Now lullay, my sweeting,
There is nothing to fear.
It is only the wind
In the willows we hear,
And the sigh of the waves
On the sand dunes, my dear.
Stay thy wailing. Let sleep be
Thy solace, thou dear;
And dreams that shall charm
From that cheek every tear.
See, see, I am with thee,
No harm can come near.
Sleep, sleep, then, my loved one,
My lorn one, my dear!"

THE CHART

That grave small face, but twelve hours here,
Maps secrets stranger than the seas',
In hieroglyphics more austere,
And older far than Rameses'.

TO A CANDLE

Burn stilly, thou; and come with me.
I'll screen thy rays. Now . . . Look, and see,
Where, like a flower furled,
Sealed from this busy world,
Tranquil brow, and lid, and lip,
One I love lies here asleep.

Low upon her pillow is
A head of such strange loveliness—
Gilded-brown, unwoven hair—
That dread springs up to see it there:
Lest so profound a trance should be
Death's momentary alchemy.

Venture closer, then. Thy light
Be little day to this small night!
Fretting through her lids it makes
The lashes stir on those pure cheeks;
The scarcely-parted lips, it seems,
Pine, but in vain, to tell her dreams.

Every curve and hollow shows
In faintest shadow—mouth and nose;
Pulsing beneath the silken skin
The milk-blue blood rills out and in:
A bird's might be that slender bone,
Magic itself to ponder on.

[33]

Time hath spread its nets in vain;
The child she was is home again;
Veiled with Sleep's seraphic grace.
How innocent yet how wise a face!
Mutely entreating, it seems to sigh,—
"Love made me. It is only I.

"Love made this house wherein there dwells
A thing divine, and homeless else.
Not mine the need to ponder why
In this sweet prison I exult and sigh.
Not mine to bid you hence. God knows
It was for joy he shaped the rose."

See, she stirs. A hand at rest
Slips from above that gentle breast,
White as winter-mounded snows,
Summer-sweet as that wild rose . . .
Thou lovely thing! Ah, welladay!
Candle, I dream. Come, come away!

SAFETY FIRST

Do not mention this young child's beauty as he stands there
    gravely before you;
Whisper it not, lest there listeners be. Beware, the evil eye!
Only as humming-bird, quaffing the delicate glory
Of the flow'r that it lives by—gaze: yes, but make no reply
To the question, What is it? Whence comes it, this
    innocent marvel?
Those features past heart to dissever from the immanent truth
    they imply?
No more than the star of the morning its image in reflex
    can ponder
Can he tell of, delight in, this beauty and promise. Oh, sigh
    of a sigh;
Be wise. Let your love through thought's labyrinths
    happily wander;
Let your silence its intricate praises, its gratitude squander;
But of speech, not a word: just a smile. Beware of the evil eye!

THE BLIND BOY

A spider her silken gossamer
In the sweet sun began to wind;
The boy, alone in the window-seat,
    Saw nought of it. He was blind.

By a lustre of glass a slender ray
Was shattered into a myriad tints,—
Violet, emerald, primrose, red—
    Light's exquisite finger-prints.

Unmoved, his face in the shadow stayed,
Rapt in a reverie mute and still.
The ray stole on; but into that mind
    No gemlike atom fell.

It paused to ponder upon a moth,
Snow-hooded, delicate past belief,
Drowsing, a spelican from his palm . . .
    O child of tragedy—if

Only a moment you might gaze out
On this all-marvellous earth we share! . . .
A smile stole into the empty eye,
    And features fair,

As if an exquisite whisper of sound,
Of source as far in time and space,
And, no less sovran than light, had found
    Its recompense in his face.

THE TOMTIT

Twilight had fallen, austere and grey,
The ashes of a wasted day,
When, tapping at the window-pane,
My visitor had come again,
To peck late supper at his ease—
A morsel of suspended cheese.

What ancient code, what Morse knew he—
This eager little mystery—
That, as I watched, from lamp-lit room,
Called on some inmate of my heart to come.
Out of its shadows—filled me then
With love, delight, grief, pining, pain,
Scare less than had he angel been?

Suppose, such countenance as that,
Inhuman, deathless, delicate,
Had gazed this winter moment in—
Eyes of an ardour and beauty no
Star, no Sirius could show!

Well, it were best for such as I
To shun direct divinity;
Yet not stay heedless when I heard
The tip-tap nothings of a tiny bird.

THE OWL

Owl of the wildwood I:
Muffled in sleep I drowse,
Where no fierce sun in heaven
Can me arouse.

My haunt's a hollow
In a half-dead tree,
Whose strangling ivy
Shields and shelters me.

But when dark's starlight
Thrids my green domain,
My plumage trembles and stirs,
I wake again:

A spectral moon
Silvers the world I see;
Out of their daylong lairs
Creep thievishly

Night's living things.
Then I,
Wafted away on soundless pinions
Fly;
Curdling her arches
With my hunting-cry:

A-hooh! a-hooh:
Four notes; and then,
Solemn, sepulchral, cold,
Four notes again,
The listening dingles
Of my woodland through:
A-hooh! A-hooh!
   A-hooh!

ONCE

Once would the early sun steal in through my eastern window,
      A sea of time ago;
Tracing a stealthy trellis of shadow across the pictures
      With his gilding trembling glow;
Brimming my mind with rapture, as though of some alien spirit,
      In those eternal hours
I spent with my self as a child; alone, in a world of wonder—
      Air, and light and flowers;
Tenderness, longing, grief, intermingling with bodiless beings
      Shared else with none:
How would desire flame up in my soul; with what
    passionate yearning
      As the rays stole soundlessly on!–
Rays such as Rembrandt adored, such as dwell on the
    faces of seraphs,
      Wings-folded, solemn head,
Piercing the mortal with sorrow past all comprehension. . . .

      Little of that I read
In those shadowy runes in my bedroom. But one wild notion
      Made my heart with tears overflow—
The knowledge that love unsought, unspoken, unshared,
    unbetokened,
      Had mastered me through and through:
And yet—the children we are!—that nought of its ardour
    and beauty
      Even the loved should know.

A RECLUSE

Here lies (where all at peace may be)
A lover of mere privacy.
Graces and gifts were his; now none
Will keep him from oblivion;
How well they served his hidden ends
Ask those who knew him best, his friends.

He is dead; but even among the quick
This world was never his candlestick.
He envied none; he was content
With self-inflicted banishment.
"Let your light shine!" was never his way:
What then remains but, Welladay!

And yet his very silence proved
How much he valued what he loved.
There peered from his hazed, hazel eyes
A self in solitude made wise;
As if within the heart may be
All the soul needs for company:
And, having that in safety there,
Finds its reflection everywhere.

Life's tempests must have waxed and waned:
The deep beneath at peace remained.
Full tides that silent well may be
Mark of no less profound a sea.

Age proved his blessing. It had given
The all that earth implies of heaven;
And found an old man reconciled
To die, as he had lived, a child.

"PHILIP"

A flattened orb of water his,
    Pent in by brittle glass
Through which his little jet-black eyes
    Observes what comes to pass:
I watch him, but how hard it is
    To estimate his size.

The further off he fins away
    The larger he appears,
And, having wheeled and turned about,
    Grows smaller as he nears!
The Great, we lesser folk agree,
Suffer from like propinquity.

But, great and small like Philip swim
In shallow waters, clear or dim;
    And few seem fully aware
    Whose bounty scatters ants' eggs there;
And all—O Universe!—poor souls,
Remain cooped up in finite bowls;
Whose psychic confines are, alas,
Seldom as clear as glass.

What truth, then, from the vast Beyond
Is theirs (in so minute a pond)
Concerning Space, or Space-*plus*-Time,
Or metaphysics more sublime,
Eludes, I fear, poor Philip's rhyme.

[43]

STILL LIFE

Bottle, coarse tumbler, loaf of bread,
Cheap paper, a lean long kitchen knife:
No moral, no problem, sermon, or text,
No hint of a Why, Whence, Whither, or If;
Mere workaday objects put into paint—
Bottle and tumbler, loaf and knife. . . .
And engrossed, round-spectacled Chardin's
      Passion for life.

THE OUTCASTS

The Brazen Trompe of Iron-wingèd fame
That mingleth truth with forgèd lies

Grunting, he paused. Dead-cold the balustrade.
Full-flood the river flowed, and black as night.
Amorphous bundle poised, he listening stayed,
Then peered, pushed, stooped, and watched it out of sight.

A faint, far plunge—and silence. Then the *whirr*
Menacing, stealthy, of a vast machine.
Midnight; but still the city was astir,
And clock to clock announced the old routine.

Trembling and fevered, light of heart and head,
He turned to hasten away; but stayed—to stare:
A paint-daubed woman bound for lonely bed,
Wide mouth, and sluggish gaze, and tinsel hair,

Stood watching him. "That's that," she said, and laughed.
"The dead—they tell no tales. Nor living *might*.
Nor need good money talk . . . What's more," she chaffed,
"Much better out of mind what's out of sight.

"*And—who?*" she added, shrugging, with a nod,
Callous and cold, towards the granite shelf.
"Not for the first time have I wished, by God,
That I had long since gone that way myself!" . . .

His puke-stained face twitched upwards in a smile.
"My friend," he said, "behold one who at last
From lifelong bondage is now freed a while.
The sack you saw contained, in fact, my Past.

"I was a writer—and of some repute,
(Candour, just now of all times, nothing burkes)—
Fiction, *belles lettres;* and I twanged the lute;
Yes, added poesy to my other works.

"Year after year the burden grew apace;
Fame, that old beldame, shared my bed and board;
No Christian, in his pilgrimage to grace,
Bore on his back a burden so abhorred.

"What was she?" Chiefly of mere fantasy made;
Seeming divine, but Lamia accursed.
She cared no more for me, insidious jade,
Than drunkard needs for quickening his thirst.

"Fattened on praise, she like a vampire sat,
Sucking my life-blood, having slain my youth;
And on her hated body I begat
Twenty abortions, but not one called Truth.

"Not, mind you, friend, it ever seemed that I
Spared of my sweat to conjure from my ink
What one might hope time would not falsify—
The most my heart could feel, my poor mind think.

"And yet by slow sour torturing degree
There crept the vile conviction in that I—
Victim of heinous anthropophagy—
Lived on my Self, as spider lives on fly.

"Ay, and that madam, sprawling in my sheets,
Vain beyond hell, a pride that knew no ebb,
Mistress, by Satan taught, of all deceits,
Never ceased weaving her mephitic web.

At my last gasp, my door one midnight stirred.
There showed a face there, tranquil as a dove.
As if a dream had spoken—yet no word:
With some lost ghost in me I fell in love . . .

"There came this moonless night. And, see, high tide! . . .
They say when Nature brings to fruitage twins—
At jutting thigh, at spine, or elsewise tied—
And one to'rds death his pilgrimage begins,

"Severance ends both. And that may be my fate.
But now," the grey face paled, the thin voice broke,
"I am at peace again. Myself—though late;
My last days freed from an atrocious yoke . . ."

The painted woman stared. Her glittering eyes
Weasel-wise watched him; then, to left and right,
Under the dull lead pallor of the skies,
Searched the dark bridge—but not a soul in sight . . .

[47]

ARROGANCE

I saw bleak Arrogance, with brows of brass,
Clad nape to sole in shimmering foil of lead,
Stark down his nose he stared; a crown of glass
Aping the rainbow, on his tilted head.

His very presence drained the vital air;
He sate erect—stone-cold, self-crucified;
On either side of him an empty chair;
And sawdust trickled from his wounded side.

LIKE SISTERS

There is a thicket in the wild
By waters deep and dangerous,
Where—close as loveless sisters—grow
Nightshade and the convolvulus.

Tangled and clambering, stalk and stem,
Its tendrils twined against the sun,
The bindweed has a heart-shaped leaf,
Nightshade a triple-pointed one.

The one bears petals pure as snow—
A beauty lingering but a day;
The other's, violet and gold,
Into bright berries shed away;

And these a poisonous juice distil.
Yet both are lovely too—as might
Those rival hostile sisters be:
Different as day is from the night
When darkness is its dead delight;—
As love is from unchastity.

THE DITCH

Masked by that brilliant weed's deceitful green,
No glint of the dark water can be seen
Which, festering, slumbers, with this scum for screen.

It is as though a face, as false as fair,
Dared not, by smiling, show the evil there.

THE DEAD JAY

A witless, pert, bedizened fop,
    Man scoffs, resembles you:
Fate levels all—voice harsh or sweet—
    Ringing the woodlands through:
But, O, poor hapless bird, that broken death-stilled wing,
    That miracle of blue!

LAID LOW

Nought else now stirring my sick thoughts to share,
Laid low, I watched the house-flies in the air;
Swarthy, obscene, they angled, gendering there.
And Death, who every daybreak now rode by—
Dust-muffled hoofs, lank animal, and he—
A mocking adept in telepathy,
Jerked in his saddle, and laughed into the sky . . .

"Where is this Blind Man's stable? Where, his grain?
What starved fowls peck his cobblestones between?
Where stews his hothouse? Why must shut remain
His iron-hinged door to those who may not bide—
As welcome guest may—for one night, then go?
What lacqueys they who at the windows hide?
And whose that scarce-heard traipsing to and fro?

Façade!—that reeks of nightmare-dread and gloom!
Dwale, henbane, hemlock in its courtyard bloom;
Dumb walls; the speechless silence of the tomb.
No smoke its clustered chimney-shafts emit;
No taper stars at attic window-pane;
Who enters, enters once—comes not again;
A vigilant vacancy envelops it. . . ."

So chattered boding to a menaced bed;
While in the east earth's sunrise broadened out.
Its pale light gilt the ceiling. My heart said,

"Nay, there is nought to fear"—yet shook with dread:
Wept, "Call him back!": groaned, "Ah! that eyeless head!"

Impassioned by its beauty; sick with doubt:—
"Oh God, give life!" and, "Would that I were dead!"

EUREKA

Lost in a dream last night was I.
I dreamed that, from this earth set free,
In some remote futurity
I had reached the place prepared for me:—

A vault, it seemed, of burnished slate,
Whose planes beyond the pitch of sight
Converged—unswerving, immaculate—
Bathed in a haze of blinding light;

Not of the sun, or righteousness.
No cherub here, o'er lute-string bowed,
Tinkled some silly hymn of peace,
But, *"Silence! No loitering allowed!"*

In jet-black characters I read
Incised upon the porcelain floor.
Ay, and the silence of the dead
No sentient heart could harrow more.

There, stretching far as eye could see,
Beneath that flat and leprous glare
A maze of immense machinery
Hummed in the ozoned air—

Prodigious wheels of steel and brass;
And—ranged along the un-windowed walls—
Engrossed in objects of metal and glass,
Stooped spectres, in spotless over-alls.

Knees quaking, dazed affrighted eyes,
I turned to the Janitor and cried,
"Is this, friend, Hell or Paradise?"
And, sneering, he replied,

"Terms trite as yours the ignorant
On earth, it seems, may yet delude.
Here, 'sin' and 'saint' and 'hierophant'
Share exile with 'the Good.'

"Be grateful that the state of bliss
Henceforth, perhaps, reserved for thee,
Is sane and sanative as this,
And void of fatuous fantasy.

"Here God, the Mechanist, reveals,
As only mechanism can
Mansions to match the new ideals
Of his co-worker, Man.

"On strict probation, you are now
To toil with yonder bloodless moles—
These skiagrams will show you how—
On mechanizing human souls . . ."

At this I woke: and, cold as stone,
Lay quaking in the hazardous light
      Of earth's familiar moon;
A clothes-moth winged from left to right,

[55]

A tap dripped on and on;
And there, my handmade pot, my jug
Beside the old grained washstand stood;
There, too, my once-gay threadbare rug,
The flattering moonlight wooed:
And—Heaven forgive a dream-crazed loon!—
I found them very good.

BUT, OH, MY DEAR

Hearts that too wildly beat—
Brief is their epitaph!
Wisdom is in the wheat,
Not in the chaff.
But, Oh, my dear, how rich and rare, and root-down-
deep and wild and sweet
It is to laugh!

THE FROZEN DELL

How still it is! How pure and cold
The air through which the wood-birds glide
From frost-bound tree to tree—
Veiled with so thin a mist that through
Its meshes steal that dayspring blue!

No other life. All motion gone—
As though a spectre, night being down,
Had through this darkened dingle trod
And frozen all he touched to stone.

Where art thou, mole? Where, busy ant?
Each in its earthen fastness is
As passive as the hive-bound bees,
As squirrel drowsing free from want,
And silken-snug chrysalides,
Queens of the wasps with ash-dark eyes—
Tranced exquisite complexities—
    And buds of the slumbering trees.

Yet human lovers, astray in this
Unfathomable silentness,
Into such dreamlike beauty come,
Though it seem lifeless as the tomb,
Might pause a moment here to kiss,

Their cold hands clasped; might even weep
For joy at their own ecstasy—
This crystal cage, sleep's wizardry,
    And secret as the womb.

BIRDS IN WINTER

I know not what small winter birds these are,
Warbling their hearts out in that dusky glade
While the pale lustre of the morning star
    In heaven begins to fade.

Not me they sing for, this—earth's shortest—day,
A human listening at his window-glass;
They would, affrighted, cease and flit away
    At glimpse even of my face.

And yet how strangely mine their music seems,
As if of all things loved my heart was heir,
Had helped create them—albeit in my dreams—
    And they disdained my share.

FEBRUARY

Whence is the secret of these skies,
Their limpid colours, deeper light,
That ardent dovelike tenderness,
Hinting at hidden mysteries
Beyond the reach of sight?

The risen sun's not half an hour
Earlier than on St. Lucy's Day;
And scarcely twice as long as that
In loftier arch, like opening flower,
His chariot loiters on the way;

But ev'n the rain upon the cheek
A kindlier message seems to bring;
There's sweetness in the moving air,
The stars of cold December's dark
Wheel on to their last westering;

And Earth herself this secret shares.
The sap is welling in her veins;
She to the heavens her bosom bares;
Snowdrop and crocus pierce the sod;
A brightening green the meadow stains.

And at her still, enticing call
The honeysuckle leaves untwine;
A softly-warbling thrush replies;
Mosses begem the orchard wall—
A fortnight from St. Valentine!

All this in open bliss appears;
Is it but fancy that within
The heart a resurrection stirs,
Some secret listener also hears
The hosannas of the Spring? . . .

And Oh, the wonder of a face—
Darkened by illness, grief and pain—
Love scarce can breathe its speechless Grace
When, mystery of all mysteries,
That heaven-sent life steals back again!

THESE SOLEMN HILLS

These solemn hills are silent now that night
Steals softly their green valleys out of sight;
The only sound that through the evening wells
    Is new-born lambkin's bleat;
    And—with soft rounded wings,
    Silvered in day's last light,
      As on they beat—
The lapwing's slow, sad, anguished
    Pee-oo-eet.

SHEEP

Early sunbeams shafting the beech-boles,
    An old oak fence, and in pasture deep—
Dark, and shapeless, dotting the shadows—
    A grazing and motionless flock of sheep;

So strangely still as they munched the grasses
    That I, up aloft on my 'bus, alone,
At gaze from its glass on the shimmering highway,
    Cried on myself:—"Not sheep! They are stone!"—

Sarsen outcrops shelved by the glaciers?
    An aeon of darkness, ice and snow?
Beings bewitched out of far-away folk-tales?
    Prodigies such as dreams can show? . . .

The mind—that old mole—has its hidden earthworks:
    Blake's greybeard into a thistle turned;
And, in his childhood, flocking angels
    In sun-wild foliage gleamed and burned.

Illusions . . . Yet—as my 'bus lurched onward,
    Beech trees, park-land and woodland gone,
It was not sheep in my memory lingered
    But, strangely indwelling, those shapes of stone.

THE CREEK

Where that dark water is,
A Naiad dwells,
Though of her presence
Little else
Than her own silence tells.

Her twilight is
The pictured shade
Between a dream
And the awakening made.

Stranger in beauty she must be—
Cold solemn face and eyes of green—
Than tongue could say,
Or aught that earthly
Sight hath seen.

Human touch,
Or gaze, or cry
Would ruin be
To her half-mortal frailty;
As to the surface of her stream
A zephyr's sigh.

ABSENCE

When thou art absent,
Grief only is constant,
My heart pines within me
Like the sighing of reeds
Where water lies open
To the darkness of heaven,
Voiceless, forsaken.

The bird in the forest
Where silence endureth,
The flower in the hollow
With down-drooping head—

Ah, Psyche, thy image!—
My soul breathes its homage;
But cold is this token,
Cold, cold is thy token,
When from dream I awaken,
By sorrow bestead.

THE BROOK

Here, in a little fall,
    From stone to stone,
The well-cool water drips,
    Lips, sips,
    And, babbling on,
Repeats its secret bell-clear song
    The whole day long.

From what far caverns,
From what soundless deep
Of earth's blind sunless rock
Did this pure wellspring seep—
As may some praeternatural dream
    In sleep?

THE RAINBOW

Stood twice ten thousand warriors on green grass
Ranked in that loop of running silver river,
The bright light dazzling on their steel and brass,
  Plumed helm, cuirass,
Tipped arrow, ivoried bow, and rain-soaked quiver;
And from these April clouds the blazing sun
Smote through the crystal drops of rain descending:
And, ere an instant of mere time was run,
  Or tongue could cry, *It's done!*
There spanned the east an arch all hues transcending:
Why, *then* would twice ten thousand dye the skies—
A different rainbow for each pair of eyes!
Oh, what a shout of joy might then be sent
From warrior throats, to crack the firmament!

But only a child was there—by that clear stream,
Reading a book, in shelter of a willow.
He raised his head to scan the radiant scene,
  His gaze aloof, serene,
  Smiling as if in dream;
And, sleeping, smiled again that night—his head upon his
  pillow.

THE GNOMON

I cast a shadow. Through the gradual day
Never at rest it secretly steals on;
As must the soul pursue its earthly way
    And then to night be gone.

But Oh, demoniac listeners in the grove,
Think not mere Time I now am telling of;
No. But of light, life, joy and awe and love:
    I obey the heavenly Sun.

EMPTY

The house by the sand dunes
Was bleached and dark and bare;
Birds, in the sea-shine,
Silvered and shadowed the air.

I called at the shut door,
I twirled at the pin:
Weeks—weeks of woesome tides,
The sand had drifted in.

The sand had heaped itself about
In the wefting of the wind;
And knocking never summoned ghost;
And dreams none can find

Like coins left at full of flood,
Gold jetsam of the sea.
Salt that water, bitter as love,
That will let nothing be

Unfevered, calm and still,
Like an ageing moon in the sky
Lighting the eyes of daybreak—
With a wick soon to die.

What then was shared there,
Who's now to tell?
Horizon-low the sea-borne light,
And dumb the buoyed bell.

[70]

LOVERS

There fell an hour when—as if clock
Had stayed its beat—their hearts stood still
At challenge of a single look,
Rapt, speechless, irretrievable.

Once, before lips had dreamed of kissing,
They languished, mind and soul, to see
Each the loved other's face; that missing,
In no wise else at peace could be.

Sleep, wherein not even dreams intrude,
Heart's haven may be from all that harms;
'Twere woe to the selfless solitude,
They find in one another's arms.

Fantastic miracle, that even,
Though now all else is nothing worth,
Would sacrifice the hope of heaven
    While love is theirs on earth!

"SAID FLORES"

"If I had a drop of attar
And a clot of wizard clay,
Birds we would be with wings of light
And fly to Cathay.

"If I had the reed called Ozmadoom,
And skill to cut pen,
I'd float a music into the air—
You'd listen, and then . . .

"If that small moon were mine for lamp,
I would look, I would see
The silent thoughts, like silver fish,
You are thinking of me.

"There is nothing upon grass or ground,
In the mountains or the skies,
But my heart faints in longing for,
And the tears drop from my eyes.

"And if I ceased from pining—
What buds were left to blow?
Where the wild swan? Where the wood-dove?
Where *then* should I go?"

NOT ONE

Turn your head sidelong;
    Gentle eyelids close;
In their small darkness
    Be all night's repose;
Weaving a dream—strange
    Flower and stranger fruit—
Wake heart may pine for
    But the day gives not.

Rest, folded lips,
    Their secret word unsaid;
Slumber will shed its dews,
    Be comforted:
Whilst I my vigil keep,
    And grieve in vain
That not the briefest moment—yours or mine—
    Can ever come again.

THE BRIBE

Ev'n should I give you all I have,—
From harmless childhood to the grave;
Call back my firstborn sigh, and then
Rob heaven of my last *Amen;*
Even if travailing back from Styx,
I brought you Pilate's crucifix;
Or, lone on Lethe, dredged you up
Melchior's golden Wassail cup;
Or Maacha's jewelled casket where
She shrined a lock of Absalom's hair;
Or relic whereon Noah would brood—
Keepsake of earth before the Flood;
Or flower of Adam's solitude;
The smile wherewith unmemoried Eve
Awoke from sleep, her fere to give,
And he, enravished, to receive;
Yes, and the daisy at her foot
She gazed at, and remembered not:
Nay, all Time's spoil, in dust put by,
Treasure untold to glut the eye—
Pining, and wonder, and mystery,
Rare and precious, old and strange,
Whithersoever thought can range,
Fish can swim, or eagle fly,
Harvesting earth, and sea, and sky;

And yours could be the empery:—
What use?
There is no power or go-between or spell in time or space
Can light with even hint of love one loveless human face.

NOT YET

"Not love me? Even yet!"—half-dreaming, I
    whispered and said.
Untarnished, truth-clear eyes; averted, lovely head:
It was thus she had looked and had listened—how often—
    before she was dead.

DIVIDED

Two spheres on meeting may so softly collide
They stay, as if still kissing, side by side.
Lovers may part for ever—the cause so small
Not even a lynx could see a gap at all.

TREASURE

Reason as patiently as moth and rust
    May fret life's ardours into dust;
But soon—the sun begins to shine, and then—
Undaunted weeds!—they up, they spread, they're all in bloom
    again.

CUPID KEPT IN

When life's wild noisy boys were out of school,
And, for his hour, the usher too was gone,
Peering at sun-fall through the crannied door,
I saw an urchin sitting there alone.

His shining wings lay folded on his back,
Between them hung a quiver, while he sat,
Bare in his beauty, and with poring brows
Bent o'er the saddening task-work he was at.

Which means she?—"*Yes or No?*" his problem was.
A gilding ray tinged plume and cheek and chin;
He frowned, he pouted, fidgeted, and wept—
Lost, mazed; unable even to begin!

But then, how could (Oh, think, my dear!), how *could*
That little earnest but unlettered mite
Find any meaning in the heart whose runes
Have kept me tossing through the livelong night?

What wonder, then, when I sighed out for shame,
He brought his scribbled slate, tears in his eyes,
And bade me hide it, until you have made
The question simpler, or himself more wise?

SCHOLARS

Logic does well at school;
And Reason answers every question right;
Poll-parrot Memory unwinds her spool;
And Copy-cat keeps Teacher well in sight:

The Heart's a truant; nothing does by rule;
Safe in its wisdom, is taken for a fool;
Nods through the morning on the dunce's stool;
And wakes to dream all night.

THOU ART MY LONG-LOST PEACE

Thou art my long-lost peace;
All trouble and all care,
Like winds on the ocean cease—
Leaving serene and fair
The evening-gilded wave
Above the unmeasured deep—
When those clear grave dark eyes
Call to the soul, in sleep—

In sleep. The waking hour—
How sweet its power may be!
Lovely the bird, the flower,
That feigns Reality!
But further yet, there is
A spirit, strange to earth,
Within whose longing lies
What day can not bring forth.

So I, though hand and lip,
Being body's, pine for thine,
Watch from my dreams in sleep
What earthly clocks resign
To cloaked Eternity:
Then weeping, sighing, must go
Back to his haunt in me,
In rapture; and in woe.

THE UNDERCURRENT

What, do you suppose, we're in this world for, sweetheart?
What—in this haunted, crazy, beautiful cage—
Keeps so many, like ourselves, poor pining human creatures,
As if from some assured, yet witholden heritage?
Keeps us lamenting beneath all our happy laughter,
Silence, dreams, hope for what may *not* come after,
While life wastes and withers, as it has for all mortals,
      Age on to age, on to age?

Strange it would be if the one simple secret
Were, that wisdom hides, as beauty hides in pebble, leaf and
    blade;
That a good beyond divining, if we knew but where to seek it,
Is awaiting revelation when—well, *Sesame* is said;
That what so frets and daunts us ev'n in all we love around us
Is the net of worldly custom which has penned us in and
    bound us;
      That—freed—our hearts would break for joy
      Arisen from the dead.

      Would "break"? What do I say?
Might that secret, if divulged, all we value most bewray!
      Make a dream of our real,
      A night of our day,
      That word said?
Oh, in case that be the answer, in case some stranger call us,
      Or death in his stead;
      Sweet Nought, come away, come away!

OUTER DARKNESS

"The very soul within my breast . . ."
"Mute, motionless, aghast . . ."

Uncompanioned, forlorn, the shade of a shade,
From all semblance of life I seemed to have strayed
To a realm, and a being—of fantasy made.
Where the spirit no more invokes Reason to prove
An illusion of sense it is cognizant of.
    I was lost: but aware.
    I had traversed the stream
By that nebulous bridge which the waking call dream,
And was come to an ultimate future that yet
Was the dust of a past no remorse could forget—
    Heart, could covet no more,
        Nor forget.

Wheresoever my eyes might forebodingly range
They discerned the familiar disguised as the strange,—
Relics of memoried objects designed
To enchant to distraction an earth-enthralled mind,
        A sense-shackled mind.
The door was ajar when I entered. And lo!
A banquet prepared for one loved, long ago.
But I shunned to peer close, to detect what was there,
As I stood, lost in reverie, facing that chair.
In anguish and dread I dared not surmise
What fate had befallen those once ardent eyes,

The all-welcoming hands, the compassionate breast,
 And the heart now at rest,
  Ev'n from love now at rest.

The glass she had drunk from beamed faintly. Its lees
Were as dry as the numberless sands of the seas
In a lunar volcano parched up by the sun
Ere the Moon's frenzied courtship of Earth had begun.
Once, the flame of that candle had yearned to retrace
The heart-breaking secrets concealed in her face—
 Gentle palace of loveliness: avid to steep
With its motionless radiance cheek, brow and lip;
And in innocent scrutiny striving to win
Through the windows now void to the phantom within,
 To the spirit secluded within.

Now its refuse was blackened. The brass of its stick—
The virginal wax guttered down to the wick—
Was witch-hued with verdigris. Fret-moth and mouse
 Had forsaken for ever this house.
As I moved through the room I was frosted with light;
 Decay was here Regent of Night.
It clotted the fabric of curtain and chair
Like a luminous mildew infesting the air;
An aeon had waned since there fell the faint call
Of the last mateless insect at knock in the wall.
The once rotten was dry—gone all sense of its taint;
The mouldings were only the shell of their paint,

Though their valueless gold
  Glimmered on, as of old:
So remote was this hush: where none listens or hears;
By all sweetness deserted for measureless years,
  The wilderness mortals call years.

    And I?
And I? Ghost of ghost, unhousel'd, foredone—
Candle, fleet, fire—out of memory gone.
Appalled, I peered on in the glass at the face
Of a creature of dread, lost in time, lost in space,
Pilgrim, waif, outcast, abandoned, alone,
In a sepulchred dark, mute as stone.
Yet of beauty, past speech, was this region of Nought
And the reflex of images conjured by thought—
Those phantoms of flow'rs in their pitcher of glass
Shrined a light that no vision could ever surpass.
In that sinister dusk every leaf, twig and tree
Wove an intricate web of significancy;
And those hills in the moonlight, a somnolent green,
Still awakened a yearning to scan the unseen,
  To seek haven within the unseen.

Alas, how can anguish and grief be allayed
  In a soul self-betrayed?
Yet that emblem of Man, in its niche by the door,
Limned a passionate pathos unheeded of yore,
A wonder, a peace, disregarded before,
  A grace that no hope could restore.

[85]

I had drunken of death. The night overhead
Was a forest of quietude, stagnant as lead;
Starless, tranquil, serene as the dead;
   The last love-stilled look of the dead.
Cold, as the snow of swan in her sleep
On pitiless Lethe to heart and to lip,
Was the void that enwrapped me—by slumber betrayed;
   Ecstatic, demented, afraid:
In a zero, forsaken, marooned: not a sigh.
An existence denuded of all but an I;
   And those relics near by:
   Neither movement nor sigh.
Till a whisper within, like a breath from the tomb,
Asked me, "Knowest thou not wherefore thus thou art come
   To this judgement, this doom?"
And my heart in my dreams stayed its pulsings: "Nay, why?"

   But Nothingness made no reply.

OUT OF A DREAM

Out of a dream I came—
Woeful with sinister shapes,
Hollow sockets aflame,
The mouth that gapes
With cries, unheard, of the dark;
The bleak, black night of the soul;
Sweating, I lay in my bed,
Sick of the wake for a goal.

And lo—Earth's close-shut door,
Its panels a cross, its key
Of common and rusting iron,
Opened, and showed to me
A face—found; lost—of old:
Of a lifetime's longing the sum;
And eyes that assuaged all grief:
     "Behold! I am come."

JOY

This little wayward Boy
Stretched out his hands to me,
Saying his name was Joy;
Saying all things that seem
Tender, and wise, and true
Never need fade while he
Drenches them through and through
With his sweet mastery;
Told me that Love's clear eyes
Pools were without the sky,
Earth, without paradise,
Were he not nigh;
Even that grief conceals
Him in a dark disguise;
And that affliction brings
    All it denies.

Not mine to heed him then—
Till felt the need—and Oh,
All his sweet converse gone,
Where could I go?
What could I do?—
But seek him up and down,
Thicket and thorn and fell,
Till night in gloom came on
Unpierceable?

Then, when all else must fail,
Stepped from the dark to me,
Voiced like the nightingale,
Masked, weeping, he.

THE VISION

O starry face, bound in grave strands of hair,
Aloof, remote, past speech or thought to bless—
Life's haunting mystery and the soul's long care,
Music unheard, heart's utter silentness,
Beauty no mortal life could e'er fulfil,
Yet garnered loveliness of all I see,
Which in this transient pilgrimage is still
Steadfast desire of that soul's loyalty;

Death's haunting harp-string, sleep's mandragora,
Mockery of waking and the dark's despair,
Life's changeless vision that fades not away—
O starry face, bound in grave strands of hair!
Hands faintly sweet with flowers from fields unseen,
Breasts cold as mountain snow and far waves' foam,
Eyes changeless and immortal and serene—
Spent is this wanderer, and you call him home!

WHITENESS

I stay to linger, though the night
Is draining every drop of light
From out the sky, and every breath
I breathe is icy chill as death.
Not so much colour now there shows
As tinges even the palest rose;
Nor in this whiteness can be seen
The faintest trace of hidden green.
Scarlet would cry as shrill as fife
Here where there stirs no hint of life.
A child in rare vermilion,
Come out to wonder at the snow,
Like Moses' burning bush would show:
Its bonfire out, when he is gone!

Yet in this pallor every tree
A marvel is of symmetry,
As if enthralled by its own grace—
A music woven of silentness.
Dense hoarfrost clots the tresses of
That weeping elm's funereal white,
Biding the sepulchre of night
To whisper,—"It is cold, my love!"
To Winter, witless nihilist,
Who, the day long, has kept his tryst
With mistress no less mute than he,
And tranced in a like rhapsody.

[91]

As though from vacant vaults of space
Darkness transfigured haunts his face;
And, she, for spell to wreathe her brow,
Has twined the Druid mistletoe.

What viol in this frozen air
Could for their nuptials descant make?
What timbrels Eros bid awake?
Ask of those solemn cedars there!

SOLITUDE

When the high road
Forks into a by-road,
And that drifts into a lane,
And the lane breaks into a bridle-path,
A chace forgotten
Still as death,
And green with the long night's rain;
Through a forest winding on and on,
Moss, and fern, and sun-bleached bone,
Till only a trace remain;
And that dies out in a waste of stone
A bluff of cliff, vast, trackless, wild,
Blue with the harebell, undefiled;
Where silence enthralls the empty air,
Mute with a presence unearthly fair,
And a path is sought
In vain. . . .

It is then the Ocean
Looms into sight,
A gulf enringed with a burning white,
A sea of sapphire, dazzling bright;
And islands,
Peaks of such beauty that
Bright danger seems to lie in wait,
Dread, disaster, boding fate;
And soul and sense are appalled thereat;

Though an Ariel music on the breeze
Thrills the mind with a lorn unease,
Cold with all mortal mysteries.
   And every thorn,
   And weed, and flower,
  And every time-worn stone
A challenge cries on the trespasser:
   Beware!
   Thou art alone!

THE UNRENT PATTERN

I roved the Past—a thousand thousand years,
Ere the Egyptians watched the lotus blow,
Ere yet Man stumbled on his first of words,
Ere yet his laughter rang, or fell his tears;
And on a hillside where three trees would grow—
    Life immortal, Peace, and Woe:
    Dismas, Christ, his bitter foe—
Listened, as yesterday, to the song of birds.

DUST

Sweet sovereign lord of this so pined-for Spring,
How breathe the homage of but one poor heart
With such small compass of thy everything?

Ev'n though I knew this were my life's last hour,
It yet would lie, past hope, beyond my power
One instant of my gratitude to prove,
    My praise, my love.

That "Everything"!—when this, my human dust,
    Whereto return I must,
Were scant to bring to bloom a single flower!

The End, he scrawled, and blotted it. Then eyed
Through darkened glass night's cryptic runes o'erhead.
"My last, and longest book." He frowned; then sighed:
    "And everything left unsaid!"

THE TRAVELLER

THE TRAVELLER

*" 'I saw that the universe is not composed of dead matter, but is . . . a
living presence.' "*

"Le soir vient; et le globe à son tour s'éblouit
    Devient un œil énorme et regarde la nuit . . ."

*"Not in lone splendour hung aloft the night
    But watching . . ."*

This Traveller broke at length to'rd set of sun,
Out from the gloom of towering forest trees;
Gasped, and drew rein. To gaze in wonder, down
A bow-shaped gulf of shelving precipices.

The blue of space dreamed level with his eye;
A league beneath, like lava long at rest,
Lay a vast plateau smooth as porphyry,
Its huge curve gradual as a woman's breast.

In saline marshes Titicaca lies,
Its City fabulous ere the Incas reigned:
Was this the like? A mountain sea? His eyes
Watched like a lynx. It still as death remained.

Not the least ripple broke the saffron sheen
Cast by th' sun across this wild abyss.
Far countries he had roved, and marvels seen,
But never such a prodigy as this.

No. Water never in a monstrous mass
Rose to a summit like a rounded stone,
Ridged with concentric shadows. No morass
Were vast as this, or coloured zone by zone.

Vague relics haunted him of mythic tales
Printed in books, or told him in his youth—
Deserts accursed, 'witched islands, sunken bells,
Fissures in space . . . Might one yet prove the truth?

Or, in his own sole being long confined,
Had he been lured into those outskirts where
A secret self is regent; and the mind
Reveals an actual none else can share?
Or had he now attained the true intent
Of his unbroken pilgrimage? The sum
Of all his communings, and what they meant?
Was life at length to its Elysium come?

So flows experience: the vast Without—
Its microcosm, of the soul, within;
Whereof the day-lit eye may be in doubt,
But doubts no more as soon as dreams begin.

Thus mused this Traveller. Was he man or ghost?
Deranged by solitude? Or rapt away
To some unpeopled limbo of the lost—
Feint that would vanish with the light of day?

In view of this huge void he camped for days,
Months of slow journeying from the haunts of men;
Till awe of it no longer could amaze,
And passion for venturing urged him on again.

Down, down into the abysm his mare, on hooves
Nimble as mountain-bred gazelle's, pricked on
From steep to steep, until through bouldered grooves
And shallowing streams she trod, the day nigh done—

An Arab lean and sleek, her surf-like mane
Tossed on a shoulder as of ivory made;
Full in the moonrise she approached the plain,
Was, with her master, in its beams arrayed.

He knew that lunar landscape from of old,
When at a window as a child he had sat—
The Face, the Thorns, the craters grisly cold,
Volcanic seas now parched and desolate;

While in the shades the bird of night bewailed
Her cruel ravishment. Ev'n then he had pined,
Ere hope abandoned him, or courage failed,
To seek adventure, safety left behind.

Chilled by his journey in the shrewd clear air,
With wind-strewn kindling-wood he built a fire;
Scant pasturage for man or beast was there,
And dreams but transiently assuage desire.

[103]

His supper done, he crouched beside the blaze,
Sharp-cheeked, wide-browed, and lost in reverie;
Flamelight and moonshine playing on his face,
The crackle of logs his only company.

When the dark tent of night at daybreak wanned
He rose, remounted, and surveyed the vast
Convex of bloodshot stone that swept beyond
In arc enormous to the skies at last.

Great mountains he had ranged that lift their snow
In peaks sublime, which age to age remain
Unstirred by foot or voice; but here, a slow
Furtive foreboding crept into his brain

Of what yet lay before him. This Unknown—
In subtle feature so unlike the past
Havens of exile he had made his own,
Been restive in, or wearied of at last.

When, soon, the climbing sun rilled down its heat,
A dewy mist, in this huge hollow pent,
Washed like a sea of milk his Arab's feet.
And rainbows arched before him as he went.

The call of waters kept his ears a-cock—
Creeks fed by cataracts now left behind.
Forests of fungus in the lichened rock
Showed spectral yellow and grey as withy-wind;

Spawn of a gendering hour, yet hoar with age,
They stood sun-bleached, ephemera of the night,
And—thing all but past speculation strange—
Growths alien until now to human sight.

What tinier atomies of life were bred
Beneath their skin-thin gills, tents, muted bells,
Eye could not guess—as procreant a bed
As is man's body with its countless cells.

The furtive mist, these clustered funguses—
Minutest stirrings of primeval slime—
The empty heavens, aloof and measureless,
Illusions seemed, not only of space, but time.

From microscopical to the immense—
Mere magnitude of little moment is;
But violent contrast shakes man's confidence
Even in what lies plain before his eyes.

Birds of rare flight and hue, of breed unknown,
Rose, wheeled, fled onward, mewling as they went—
And left him—more forsaken and alone,
Sun for sole guidance in his slow ascent.

But borne not far upon the windless air,
The fickle fleet-winged creatures turned anon;
Came stooping backward on his face to stare:
Broke out in cries again; again, were gone:

[105]

Curious, but fearless of what never yet
Had on these mighty slopes been seen to appear;
With soft-tongued jargoning they his way beset,
Sadder than love-lorn pewit's on the ear.

Nor was it only stone that made reply;
Their sweetness echoed in his heart; delight,
And love, long pent in fadeless memory
Welled to his eyes. He watched them out of sight.

Eastward to westward, wide as gaze could scan,
Shallowly troughed the bare savanna swept:
The dead of all the armies doomed by Man
Could, biding Judgement, in its folds have slept.

And hollow as sinister beating of a drum
The rock resounded when, with sudden bound,
His beast beneath him, on the treacherous scum,
Slipped, and with snort of fear, her balance found.

That night, while yet in darkness lapped, it seemed
He had leapt from sleep, that instant made aware
The rock beneath had trembled while he dreamed
Bleached of a sudden by the lightning's glare.

Boding of perils unconceived before,
He woke when dawn again suffused the sky.
His earth, once stable, now proved insecure,
He sat and watched it with unwinking eye;

While chattering voices wrangled in his head:
"Alas, what horror of the soul is this?"
"Beware! Away!" "Far better thou were dead
Than face the ordeal that now before thee lies!"

A plaintive whinny in the early air,
For company calling, solace brought. He smiled.
And in sweet converse with his timorous mare
Soothed her disquiet, and his own beguiled.

Towards noon an arid wind from out the East
Waxed, waned; and failed as they approached—these two.
In close companionship of man and beast,
To where the plain they paced lapsed into blue.

His dazzled eyes rejoiced. No more there showed
Branched veins of sanguine in a milk-pale stone;
An ever deepening azure gloomed and glowed
In shine and shadow as they journeyed on:

Turquoise, and sapphire, speedwell, columbine.
When clouds minute like scales of fish are seen
Bedappling April daybreak, then, divine
As Eros' eyes, there shows a blue between,

Tranquil, wan, infinite. So, pale to dark,
A dark as dazzling as the tropic deep,
Loomed now the prospect toward his distant mark,
When yet again he laid him down to sleep.

In this oblivion he dreamed a dream:—
He dreamed the transitory host of men,
Debased by pride, lust, greed and self-esteem,
Had gone their way; that Earth was free again.

Their minds had brewed a poison in their blood;
The sap of their own nature had decayed.
They had chosen evil, had resigned the good;
False, faithless, pitiless, and of nought afraid.

Nature, released from this vile incubus,
Had wooed into being creatures of other kind,
Resembling those long since deemed fabulous,
As exquisite in aspect as in mind;

Beings, too, once adored for beauty and grace,
Who had left but echoes in the mirroring air,
Had sought again this bygone dwelling-place,
As happy birds in April homeward fare.

And he?—the sport of contraries in sleep!—
To childhood had returned, gone grief and woe;
That Eden of the heart, and fellowship
With innocence, that only children know;

And in a garden played, serene, alone;
Bird, flower, water shining in his eyes,
And magic hidd'n in even the tiniest stone . . .
When, suddenly, a Trumpet rent the skies:

[108]

To Judgement had been called the Sons of Light,
The stellar host, the Sun and all his brood:
Rank beyond rank, height above heavenly height,
Within the eternal peace of God they stood,

Hymning his glory. And, alas, he knew
That, chosen envoy of the earth, he had come,
Garbed in her beauty, and enraptured too;
But, though he had yearned for joy, his soul was dumb.

And by unuttered edict exiled thence,
He had fallen, as Satan fell, in leaden dismay,
And thus had wakened to the rock-land whence
His spirit, in fantasy, had winged away.

Heartsick he turned to scan the heights remote
Long left behind, their groves of slumbrous green;
No frailest wisp of vapour lay afloat
Dawn's rose-flushed void pavilion within.

Long time he sate, night's pageant in his mind,
Doubting his senses, vacantly aware
Of what already instinct had divined—
His deadliest danger now was blank despair.

Like some old zany, he seemed, who, year by year,
The slave has been of an *Excelsior,*
Its goal *Eureka;* and when that draws near
Hears fleshless knuckles on his chamber-door!

[109]

Or like a doting lover who at last
By one whose source had seemed of heavenly grace
Forsaken is, in outer darkness cast,
This cheating blandishment a Lamia's face.

Meagre his saddlebag as camel's hump
When, sand-marooned, she staggers to her doom.
As shrunken too, his Arab's meagre rump
Showed taut as vellum stretched upon a drum.

He strove in vain to reason, numbed with sleep,
But conscious that at first faint token of dawn,
Wraiths at whose beauty even the blind might weep,
Wooed to his solitude, had come, and gone—

Wraiths all but lost to memory, whose love
Had burned in hearts that never more would beat
Of whose compassion sense could bring no proof,
Though solace 'twas beyond all telling sweet!—

Like flowers that a child brings home; to fade.
Alas, alas, no longing could restore
Life to the faithful by neglect betrayed!
Too late for ransom; they'd return no more—

Had left him, like a castaway adrift,
Lashed to a raft upon a chartless sea,
His only motion the huge roller's lift,
Its depths his only hope at peace to be.

"Sea!" when this waste of stone where now he lay
Like polished porcelain was, untinged with red.
But when his cracked lips stirred, as if to pray,
He caught but leaf-dry whisper of what they said.

So tense was this, his solitude—the sky
Its mute and viewless canopy—that when
His grieved "O God!" was followed by a sigh,
It seemed Eternity had breathed *Amen*.

Ay, as if cock, horizon-far, had crowed,
His heart, like Peter's, had been rent in twain.
At pang of it his grief again up-flowed
Though its *Who's there?* called only in his brain . . .

On, and still on he pressed—scorched heel to nape,
Hunched in his saddle from the noonday's glare—
Watched by a winged thing, high in heaven, agape
To ken aught stirring in a tract so bare,

Which leaf or blade of grass could never yield:
A vitreous region, like a sea asleep,
Crystalline, convex, tideless and congealed,
Profounder far than Tuscarora Deep,

Further than sight could reach before him lay.
Head bent, eyes fixed—drowsed by recurrent stroke
Of tic-tac ice-like hoof-beats, famished, fey,
He slipped again from real to dream: awoke

To find himself marooned beneath a dome
Of star-pricked vacancy, and darkness near;
His breast bespattered with his Arab's foam,
And—trotting at his heels—the spectre, *Fear.*

This fell pursuit, unhastening, pace for pace—
Like *lama* of Tibet in waking trance—
His very soul for quarry in the chase,
Forbade all hazard of deliverance:

A mantled shape of horror mildew-blue,
With naked feet, blank eyes, and flattened face,
Insane with lust, that ever nearer drew,
Tarrying for midnight and the dread embrace.

Foes of the soul there are, corrupt, malign,
Taint of whose malice is so evil a blight
That ev'n the valiant must hope resign
Unless God's mercy give them means for flight.

Witless as wild bird tangled in a net,
He dared not turn his head, but galloped on,
Spurs red at heel, his body drenched with sweat,
Until, with nerve renewed, but strength nigh gone,

He slowed his pace to listen; gasped, fordone;
Drew rein, dismounted. But the peril past
His face was fallen in like that of one
Whom mortal stroke of fate has felled at last;

And in a moment aged him many years—
Edict beyond the mind to comprehend.
Plaiting cramped fingers in the elf-locked mane,
"Come, now," he muttered, "we must rest, my friend."

The creature's sunken eyeballs, scurfed with rheum
And dimmed with misery, returned his gaze;
And thus they communed in the gathering gloom,
Nought but the love between them left to graze.

She pawed the unnatural ice, tossed her small head,
By inarticulate alarm distressed;
Baring her teeth squealed faintly, smitten with dread;
And, snuggling closer, lipped her master's breast.

"Quiet, dear heart! The end is nearing now.
Into disaster thou hast been betrayed."
He smoothed her gentle muzzle, kissed her brow.
"Nought worse than one more night to live," he said.

"We both are mortal, and have fallen at last
Into disgrace. But had I swerved aside,
And safety chosen, what peace, the danger past,
Is his who sleeps with Terror for his bride?

"Only one night. And then must come what may.
But never mistress held man's life in fee
As mine has been. And how could speech convey
The grief, forlorn one, that I feel for thee!"

[113]

So mourned he in his heart. This comrade dear!
His gentle hand upon her shoulder lay
Though still she shivered, twitching flank and ear,
In this drear sterile waste so far astray.

Long stood he motionless, while overhead
The circling constellations east to west,
Misting the infinite, their influence shed—
Friends long familiar on how many a quest!

From this far timeless quiet of the mind
It seemed an inward voice had summoned him:—
"See! See!"—a whisper fainter than the wind
Or ripple of water lipped on Lethe's brim.

For now—the zenith darkening—opal-pale,
As if the earth its secret well-spring were—
Softly as flowers of night their scents exhale,
A strange and deepening lustre tinged the air,

Gentle and radiant. So, from off the sea,
May mirrored moonbeams, when calm waters lave
A rock-bound coast, steal inward silently,
Blanching the sombre vaultings of a cave.

Not rock his roof-tree here, but hollow sky;
Not reflex moon-ray, but a spectral light,
Like hovering, pervasive Reverie
Of mind supreme, illumining the night.

Awed by this loveliness, his spellbound face,
To travail, the while, and anguish reconciled,
Of fret and weariness shed every trace—
As sleep brings comfort to a tired-out child:

Sleep to a body, so pure and exquisite,
Like manna it is at gilding sunrise seen,
The senses so untrammeled that as yet
No more than frailest barrier lies between

Soul and reality. Thus beauty may
Pierce through the mists that worldly commerce brings,
Imagination's blindness wash away,
And—bird at daybreak—lend the spirit wings.

Even the busy ant, devoid of fear,
Prowling beneath the shadow of a man,
Conscious may be of occult influence near,
Whose origin it neither recks, nor can.

So, though he too was now but vaguely aware
Whence welled this boon of benison and peace,
In awe of a presence so divinely fair,
Tears gushed within him, not of grief but bliss.

Courage revived—like greenness after rain.
Slowly he turned; looked back. And in amaze—
A waif self-exiled from the world of men—
Trembled at sight of what now met his gaze:—

The hushed and visionary host of those
Who, like himself, had faced life's long duress,
Its pangs and horrors, anguish, hardship, woes,
Their one incentive ever on to press,

Defying dread and danger—and in vain:
Not to achieve a merely temporal goal,
Not for bright glory, praise, or greed of gain,
But in that secret craving of the soul

For what no name has; flow'r of hidden stem:—
The unreturned of kindless land and sea;
Venturers, voyagers, dreamers, seers—ay, them
The Angel of Failure hails with rhapsody.

Him, too, for some rare destiny designed
Who, in faith and love, has ranged; unmarked, alone;
Though means to share it he will never find
Since its sole language is unique—his own.

Ay, what though Man have but one earthly life,
Cradle to grave, wherein to joy and grieve?
His grace were yet the agony and strife
In quest of what no mortal can achieve.

"*Angel,*" forsooth! Bleak visage, frigid breast,
Passionless Nemesis, the heart for prey,
She goads her votary with insane unrest
And smiles upon him when she stoops to slay.

[116]

Strange beauty theirs, this host, starved, marred, forlorn
In mien and aspect. Rapt, intent, and dumb,—
Laved in light lovely as the primal morn,—
They brought their homage to his Kingdom Come.

Less a mere castaway of flesh and bone,
Defenceless, lost, whom Fate will overwhelm,
He now appeared, than—child of genius—one
Who explores pure Fantasy's unbounded realm;

And being at length confronted by ordeal
No human consciousness could comprehend,
A superhuman ecstasy can feel—
Life's kiss of rapture at life's journey's end.

"All hail!" he muttered; paused; then laid him low,
His crazed head pillowed on his Arab's flank;
Prostrate with thirst and weariness and woe,
Into a plumbless deep of sleep he sank.

What visitants of earth or air drew near
Rider and horse in these brief hours of night—
Sylphs of the wilderness or demon drear,
Gazed long and softly, and again took flight,

No sense ajar revealed; nor echo of
Music ethereal, pining sweet and shrill,
Of voices in the vaults of heaven above,
The angelic solitudes of Israfel . . .

When daybreak rilled across the hushed expanse,
He woke at peace, refreshed. And though aware
Nought now could shield him from his last mischance;
With tranquil mind he breathed the scentless air.

This barren world!—no weed here raised its head;
No bird on dew-plashed wing, his ear to bless,
Flew up to greet the dayspring; but instead,
A tense unfathomable silentness

Engulfed the enormous convex, stony still,
Of hueless, lucent crystal where he lay,
Shiv'ring in fever in the sunless chill,
Its centre now scarce half a league away.

He rose; the rustle of his raiment seemed
A desecration of the quietude
Mantling its vacancy, as if there dreamed
A presence here where none had dared intrude

Since waters from waters had divided been,
World from the heavens, the land from ocean freed;
And fruitful trees sprang up, with leafage green,
And earth put forth the herb that yieldeth seed.

"Come, now," he whispered; and then stopped, aghast,
Thinking his faithful one had found reprieve;
Had fled away, all tribulation past,
Where even the soul-less languish not nor grieve;

But green-grey willows hang their tresses down;
The heron fishes in his plashy pool;
There, in her beauty floats the silver swan—
Shady and verdurous and calm and cool.

Meadows where asphodel and cowslips blow,
And sun-lit April clouds dissolve in rain—
Her earthly paradise! At length! But no;
The gentle creature heard, had stirred again.

Scrabbling her fore-hoofs on the treacherous waste,
She rose, stood trembling; with sepulchral sigh
Turned her night-blinded eyes, her master faced;
And patiently, piteously set out to die.

To eyried bird above, now rosed with light,
Of insectine dimensions they appeared;
Like woodlice creeping, or the weevil-mite
That in a mouldering ship at sea is reared.

Sable in plumage, ruff, and naked head,
Superb in flight, and poised upon his shelf
Of viewless air, he tarried for the dead,
And watched, indifferent as Death himself.

Though the great globe around them grudged them tomb,
Feast they would be for both these ravening foes—
Horseman and Arab, who had dared to roam
Beneath these mountains' never-melting snows.

Halt, maimed and impotent, still travelling on,
O'er very *Eye of Earth* they made their way,
Till rimmed into the East the risen sun
Flooding its orbit with the light of day—

So brilliant the least flaw beneath their feet
A tiny shadow threw where nought there was
Taller than locust in the dustless heat
To check the splendour of this sea of glass.

And if pure radiance could pure music be,
And quiet supreme its tabernacle were,
This orb, now blazing in his majesty,
With a sublime Hosanna rent the air.

Moved by an impulse beyond wit to scan,
His poor rags stirring in a fitful breeze,
This worn, outwearied, errant son of man
Paused, bowed his head, fell down upon his knees;

And, with a faint and lamentable cry,
Poured hoarsely forth a babble of praise and prayer,
Sun on his brows, above the boundless sky,
No living soul to hear or heed him there:

A self there is that listens in the heart
To what is past the range of human speech,
Which yet 'twould seem, has tidings to impart—
The all-but-uttered, and yet out of reach.

Beneath him an immeasurable well
Of lustrous crystal motionlessly black
Deeped on. And as he gazed—marvel past words to tell—
It seemed to him a presence there gazed back:

Rapt, immaterial, remote; ev'n less
In substance than is image of the mind;
And yet, in all-embracing consciousness
Of its own inmost being; elsewise blind:

Past human understanding to conceive,
Of primal innocence, yet source of all
That matter had the power to achieve
Ere Man created was, ere Adam's fall:

And in its midst a mote scarce visible—
Himself: the momentary looking-glass
Of Nature, which a moment will annul
And with Earth's hosts will into nothing pass:

The flux of change. Ay, this poor Traveller too—
Soon to be dust, though once in life elate,
Yet from whose gaze a flame divine burned through;
A son of God—no sport of Time or Fate.

It seemed his heart was brok'n; his whole life long
Now centred in this moment of desire;
Its woe, its rapture transient as the song
The Phoenix sings upon her funeral pyre.

"Alas!" he gasped—earth's journey now at end;
Breathed softly out his last of many sighs,
Flung forth his hands, and motionless remained,
Drenched through with day; and darkness in his eyes . . .

Head dropped, knees sagging, his forsaken jade—
Her hide now gilded by the eastern sun,
Her abject carcass in its glory arrayed,
As though in fear to break his prayers—drowsed on.

But, as an acid frets its way through steel,
Into her sentience at length there crept
A hush not ev'n this silence could conceal—
And Death for long has never secret kept,

Though shadow-close it mime its sister, Sleep.
The creature nearer drew, reluctant, slow,
As if, like motherless child, to sigh and weep,
Too young the import of its loss to know.

Ears pricked, reins dangling, thus awhile she stayed—
Of that in watch above full well aware;
"See, now, dear master, here I wait!" She neighed,
And stooping, snuffed the rags, the matted hair;

Then, of a sudden, in panic dread, upreared,
Plunged, wheeled, drew back, her eyeballs gleaming white,
And urged to frenzy by the thing she feared
From all that love had left on earth took flight . . .

Sweet is that Earth, though sorrow and woe it have
For those who travail. Comes the journey's end:
Anima mundi! and the soundless grave
No man can or foretoken or forfend.

PROBLEMS

"Gone! Where? My glasses!" the old quidnunc cries;
    And still the blinder grows,
Until (the problems life solves in this wise!)
    He finds them on his nose.

DATE DUE